About the authors:

Seiko Ogawa: She graduated from Kagawa Nutrition University. Her cooking meets the needs of the times. She writes for magazines and plays an active role in the world of advertisement.

Ine Mizuno: She lives in Chiba Prefecture. She is highly reputed to have created a variety of fancy rolled sushi. She is making every effort to work out new style of sushi.

Measurements used in this book:

Rice   1 cup = 180 cc

Others 1 cup = 200 cc

1 Tbsp (tablespoon) = 15 cc

1 tsp (teaspoon) = 5 cc

Sake, *Mirin*, and *Dashi stock* are essential to Japanese Cooking.
* *Sake* (rice wine) mellows food, tones down raw taste or smells and improves flavor. Dry sherry can be a substitute for *sake*.
* *Mirin* (sweet cooking rice wine) is used to improve flavor and give food glaze and sweetness. *Mirin* may be substituted with 1 Tbsp *sake* and 1 tsp sugar.
  Both *sake* and *mirin* are now manufactured in the USA.
* For preparations of *Dashi stock*, see inside back cover page.

NEW WAVES OF ONIGIRI

Colorful onigiri is now on the menu. Using a variety of ingredients, you can make your choice of onigiri in a Japanese, Western or Chinese style. Set the ingredients on the onigiri, mix with the rice, or sprinkle over. The methods are infinite. Show your personal sense by creating your own original onigiri.

●●

CANAPÉ-STYLE ONIGIRI

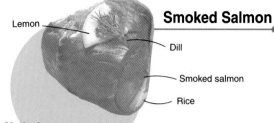

Smoked Salmon

Lemon — Dill — Smoked salmon — Rice

Method: Make a rice ball into a triangle shape with plain rice. Wrap in smoked salmon and top with a slice of lemon and a piece of dill.

Anchovy

Radish — Cottage cheese — Anchovy — Rice mixed with minced parsley

Method: ❶ Mince the parsley and mix with rice. Make a rice ball into a barrel-shaped form.
❷ Drain oil from canned anchovy. Place on top and add cottage cheese. Garnish with a slice of radish.

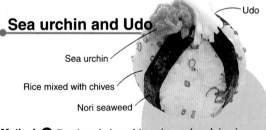

Sea urchin and Udo

Udo — Sea urchin — Rice mixed with chives — Nori seaweed

Method: ❶ Cut the udo into thin strips and soak in vinegared water.
❷ Cut the chives into pieces and mix with rice. Make a round rice ball. Bind with strips of nori seaweed crosswise.
❸ Top with the sea urchin and udo.

Sausage

Broccoli — Sausage — Rice mixed with cheese

Method: ❶ Cut processed cheese into small cubes and mix with rice and a pinch of salt. Make a flat round rice ball.
❷ Top with a slice of sausage and boiled broccoli.

Crab and Corn

Corn — Mayonnaise — Crab — Lettuce — Rice

Method: ❶ Make a flat round rice ball.
❷ Drain liquid from canned crab meat. Place it with corn on a lettuce leaf. Garnish with mayonnaise.

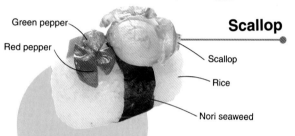

Scallop

Green pepper — Red pepper — Scallop — Rice — Nori seaweed

Method: ❶ Sauté the scallop in butter. Cut peppers into pieces and sauté in butter. Season with salt and pepper.
❷ Make a cylinder-shaped rice ball and bind with a strip of nori seaweed. Top with ①.

Minced Chicken and Thin Omelet

Minced chicken — White radish sprouts — Rice — Thin Omelet

Method: ❶ Add sugar, soy sauce, wine and juice of ginger to the minced chicken and stir-fry. Add sugar and salt to an egg and make a thin omelet.
❷ Make a triangular rice ball and wrap in the thin omelet. Top with the minced chicken and garnish with radish sprouts.

Salmon Roe

Slice of citrus fruit — Salmon roe — Rice mixed with aojiso leaves

Method: ❶ Cut aojiso (green shiso leaves) leaves into thin strips and mix with rice. Make a rice ball into a flat round shape.
❷ Dip the salmon roe in sake briefly and put on the rice ball. Garnish with a slice of citrus fruit.

Fish Onigiri

Enjoy various shapes of onigiri with fancy cutters.

Ingredients & Method: ❶ Add a pinch of salt to minced cashew nuts and mix with rice. Moisten a cutter with water and fill in with the rice mixture. Remove.

❷ Drain oil from canned sardines and place them on the rice. Top with a slice of cherry tomato and chervil.

Squid and Pickled Plum Flesh

Nigiri-zushi-like onigiri with fresh squid.

Ingredients & Method: ❶ Make a square rice ball similar to nigiri-zushi. Place aojiso (green shiso leaves) on it.

❷ Cut fresh squid into thin strips and dress with pickled plum flesh. Place it on the rice ball. Stick sheets of dried bonito around the ball.

Two-colored Onigiri

A mix of Japanese and Western styles.

Ingredients & Method: ❶ Break up cod roe on a sheet of plastic wrap. Place bite-sized rice ball on top and wrap up.

❷ Prepare another rice ball by mixing with minced parsley and a pinch of salt. Spread cream cheese on a sheet of plastic wrap. Place the rice ball on it and wrap up.

❸ Garnish with paprika and white radish sprouts. Skewer both balls.

Japanese-style Mixed Onigiri

Top with pickles, furikake (condiment for sprinkling over rice) or anything available in the refrigerator. The wrapper is tatami-iwashi (sardine paper). Tsukudani (shellfish boiled in sweetened soy sauce) and salted kombu are also good for ingredients.

Ingredients & Method: ❶ Make a flat round rice ball. Wrap tatami-iwashi around it.

❷ Top with sakuraebi (dried small shrimp), furikake (condiment for sprinkling over rice) and pickled cucumber.

Roast Pork Onigiri

Add salt to the mixture.

Ingredients & Method: ❶ Cut a shishito (hot pepper) into slices, add a pinch of salt and mix with rice. Make a flat round rice ball.
❷ Top with slices of roast pork, hard-boiled quail egg cut into halves and sprinkle with black sesame.

Cabbage Roll with Curried Rice

Wrap curried rice in cabbage and ham.

Ingredients & Method: ❶ In a pan, parch curry powder (1/3 tsp per rice ball) over low heat until it smells.
❷ Turn off the heat and add boiled rice and mix. With a little salt on the palms, make a rice ball.
❸ Boil the cabbage until soft and drain. Remove stalks and place slices of ham on it.
❹ Wrap the rice ball in the cabbage and ham. Make cuts on top. Garnish with pickled cucumber and onion, and parsley.

Fruit Onigiri

Rice is a kind of vegetable. Make a salad-like onigiri with fruits.

Ingredients & Method: ❶ With a pinch of salt on the palms, make a flat round rice ball.
❷ Top with slices of canned pineapple, kiwi fruit, plum and garnish with mint leaves.

Chestnut and Bean Onigiri

A novel onigiri with sweet ingredients.

Ingredients & Method: ❶ Soak dried shiitake in water to reconstitute it. Cut it into thin slices. Cook in the water in which the shiitake was soaked adding sugar and soy sauce added.
❷ Mix boiled rice and shiitake. With a pinch of salt on the palms, make a triangular rice ball.
❸ Top with sweet-boiled red beans and chestnuts with poppy seeds sprinkled on top.

A) SALTED SALMON

A familiar ingredient for onigiri.
Ingredients & Method: ❶ Make a rice ball into a barrel-shaped form. Wrap nori seaweed around it.
❷ Grill salted salmon and break it up. Place it on top and garnish with a small chrysanthemum.

B) KIMCHI

Korean-style onigiri with kimchi.
Ingredients & Method: ❶ Mix rice and pine nuts and make a rice ball.
❷ Drain liquid from kimchi. Cut it into strips, 3/8" (1 cm) wide. Place it on top and garnish with chive cut into pieces and fine chili pepper.

C) BROILED EEL

Savory onigiri with broiled eel.
Ingredients & Method: ❶ Make a rice ball into a long and thick shape. Wrap tangle flakes around it.
❷ Cut broiled eel to the size of onigiri and place it on top. Garnish with kinome (bud of Japanese pepper).

D) KAMABOKO

Kamaboko is boiled or steamed fish paste, which goes well with sake.
Ingredients & Method: ❶ Mix rice, black sesame seeds and a pinch of salt and make a flat round rice ball.
❷ Top with slices of kamaboko and grated horseradish. Sprinkle with a little soy sauce before eating.

E) SMOKED CHICKEN

Smoked flavor goes well with the smell of aonori seaweed.
Ingredients & Method: ❶ Make a rice ball into a flat round shape. Wrap green-seaweed flakes around it before the rice gets cool.
❷ Break up smoked chicken and place the pieces on top. Garnish with a stuffed olive.

D

H

F

G

G) WIENER

Savory almonds give accent to the rice ball.

Ingredients & Method: ❶ Roast almond slices in a moderate oven. Add a pinch of salt and mix with rice. Make a cylinder-shaped rice ball.

❷ Cut the wiener into diagonal slices. Place the sausage on top together with whole mustard and garnish with watercress.

H) TUNA

Relish the taste of oyster sauce.

Ingredients & Method: ❶ Mix rice and oyster sauce (1/2 - 1 tsp per ball) and make a round rice ball.

❷ Drain oil from tuna and break it up. Place the tuna on the rice ball together with Chinese parsley and top with a bit of tomato ketchup.

F) SHRIMP

Salty pickles will improve the flavor.

Ingredients & Method: ❶ Cut pickled greens into pieces and mix with rice. Make a rice ball into a flat round shape.

❷ Boil shrimp in salted water and shell. Together with a slice of lemon and tonburi (cooked grains of summer cypress), place the shrimp on top.

Substantial rice and side dish

SIDE-DISH ONIGIRI

CURRIED MEUNIÉRE OF WHITEFISH

Ingredients (for 4 balls)

2 steaks whitefish
1/2 tsp salt
A little pepper
{ 4 Tbsp flour
{ 1 Tbsp curry powder

4 cups cooked rice
4 lettuce leaves
1 cherry tomato
2 Tbsp oil for sautéing

Method: ❶ Cut each fish steak into 4 pieces. Sprinkle with salt and pepper and let stand to absorb taste.
❷ Mix the flour and curry powder. Pat dry fish and coat with the mixture. Discard extra powder.
❸ Heat the oil in a frying pan and sauté the fish until brown.
❹ Sandwich the fish between the cooked rice and squeeze firmly.
❺ Wrap in lettuce leaves and garnish with the tomato.

ONIGIRI WITH BEEF SHREDS

Ingredients (for 4 balls)

3 1/2 oz (100 g) thinly
  sliced beef
2 green peppers
2~3 Tbsp sauce for beef
  (store-bought)

A little cornstarch
4 cups cooked rice
4 lettuce leaves
Some white sesame seeds
2 Tbsp oil for sautéing

Method: ❶ Cut beef and peppers into julienne strips.
❷ Heat oil in a frying pan and sauté beef. When the color changes, add peppers and sauté together.
❸ Add the sauce and thicken with cornstarch dissolved in water.
❹ Place ③ on top of the rice and sprinkle with sesame seeds.

ONIGIRI WITH MINI HAMBURGERS

Ingredients (for 4 balls)

For hamburgers
- 7 oz (200 g) ground beef
- 1/2 onion
- 1/2 egg
- 1/4 cup breadcrumbs
- 2 Tbsp milk
- 1/2 tsp salt
- Dash pepper
- 2 tsp butter

- 2 Tbsp Worcester sauce
- 2 Tbsp tomato ketchup
- 4 cups cooked rice
- 4 lettuce leaves
- A little white radish sprouts
- 1 radish
- 2 Tbsp oil for sautéing

Method: ❶ Mince the onion and sauté in butter. Let it cool. Combine the other ingredients for hamburgers and mix well. Divide into 4 oval patties.

❷ Heat the oil in a frying pan and sauté the hamburgers. When cooked discard the oil, and cut in half. Add the ketchup and sauce and cook until the liquid has evaporated.

❸ Place the hamburgers on top of the rice and squeeze firmly. Garnish with slices of radish and radish sprouts.

ONIGIRI WITH PORK CUTLET

Ingredients (for 4 balls)

- 1 large pork loin steak
- A little salt and pepper
- Batter
  - A little flour
  - 1 egg
  - Proper amount of breadcrumbs to cover

- Proper amount of Worcester sauce
- 4 cups cooked rice
- 1~2 cabbage leaves
- 4 lettuce leaves
- 2 lemon slices
- Oil for deep-frying

Method: ❶ Cut cabbage leaves into julienne strips.

❷ Cut stringy membrane of pork and sprinkle with salt and pepper. Dredge with flour. Dip in the beaten egg and then the breadcrumbs.

❸ Heat the oil to 360°F (180°C). Add the pork and deep-fry until golden and crispy. Cut it into 8 portions while hot. Pour the sauce over.

❹ Place the pork and cabbage on top of the rice and squeeze firmly.

Note: You may cut the cabbage into big pieces and parboil.

VARIATIONS WITH TEMPURA

Onigiri with a shrimp tempura in the center and wrapped in nori seaweed has become popular throughout Japan. It is said that it originated in Nagoya or Tsu in Mie Prefecture.

The familiar bite-sized onigiri is attractive, but try larger onigiri with original ingredients. The gorgeous onigiri will be good to serve your guests.

● BASIC ONIGIRI WITH TEMPURA

Ingredients (for 8 balls)

8 small prawns
Condiment
{ 1/3 tsp salt
{ 1 Tbsp sake
Batter
{ 1 cup flour
{ 3/4 cup (1 egg + cold water)

8 cups cooked rice
Nori seaweed
Oil for deep-frying

PREPARATION AND DEEP-FRYING

1 Shell the prawn with the tail intact and devein with a bamboo skewer. Sprinkle with the condiment and let stand for about 30 minutes.

2 Batter: Beat the egg with cold water and then fold in the flour. Make the batter firmer than usual.

3 Pat dry the prawn. Dip in the batter and deep-fry in oil heated to 360°F (180°C) until tender-crisp.

HOW TO MAKE A RICE BALL

4 Salt hot rice. Put the prawn in the center and squeeze the rice ball with both hands.

5 Let the prawn tail stick out and wrap the rice ball in nori seaweed.

Try various shapes of rice balls. Instead of nori seaweed, you may use bonito sheets, aojiso (green shiso leaves) or shavings of tangle.

Fried prawn with parsley

Ingredients & Method: Season prawn with salt and sake. Prepare batter with flour and minced parsley. Dip the prawn in the batter and deep-fry until crisp.

Fried prawn with sesame seeds

Ingredients & Method: Add 2 Tbsp black sesame seeds to the batter on page 10. Dip prawn, seasoned with salt and sake, in the batter and deep-fry until crisp.

Fried squid with garlic

Ingredients & Method: Skin squid and season with salt and pepper. Add grated garlic to breadcrumbs. Coat the squid with breadcrumbs and deep-fry until golden brown.

Fried prawn with green seaweed

Ingredients & Method: Add green seaweed and a pinch of shichimi-togarashi (seven-spice chili pepper) to batter. Dip seasoned prawn in the batter and deep-fry until crisp.

Fried squid with yukari

Ingredients & Method: Coat seasoned squid with flour. Add a pinch of yukari (minced salted and dried shiso leaves) to batter. Dip the squid in the batter and deep-fry. Yukari is salty, so use moderately.

Fritters with shrimp

Ingredients & Method: Add seasoned shrimp and mitsuba (honewort) cut into pieces to flavored batter. Drop in heated oil and deep-fry until crunchy.

TRADITIONAL ONIGIRI

Like sandwiches for the Americans, rice balls are the most popular food in Japan for carrying along. Japanese people cherish an unforgettable memory of the onigiri prepared by their mothers when on outings or hiking. Now let's look back on the traditional taste.

BASICS OF RICE PREPARATION

WASH RICE AND SOAK IN WATER

Measure an exact amount of rice. A measuring cup of a rice cooker contains 180 cc.

Cover with water and swirl quickly to get rid of the smell of bran. Discard the first water.

Wash lightly rubbing grains of rice with your hand.

Replace water 3 to 4 times until it is no longer cloudy. If you do not wash the rice well, it will soon go bad.

Transfer the rice to a colander and drain. Let it stand for 30 minutes in summer and an hour in winter.

Cover with water according to the mark. The quantity of water is about 10% more than the rice and less for newly harvested rice.

AFTER COOKED

Well cooked rice is fluffy and the grain is glossy.

Using a wet wooden spatula, pull the rice away from the side of the cooker.

To let in air turn over the rice, making cutting and turning motions, and fluff the rice up.

HOW TO MAKE A RICE BALL

Once you acquire the knack of making rice balls, you will become the master of onigiri. It is not power, but whole-heartedness that counts for making a successful onigiri.

THE FOUR IMPORTANT POINTS

1. The quantity of rice
A bowl of cooked rice makes one rice ball. A cup of rice makes three rice balls.

2. Filling
Make a small well in the center of the rice with a finger and place ingredients inside.

3. Wet hands with water
Wet palms all over lightly with water. Too much water will spoil the rice ball.

4. The quantity of salt
Salt on tips of two fingers is enough. Don't use salt for cooked rice with other ingredients, rice mixed with yukari (minced salted and dried shiso leaves) or pickles.

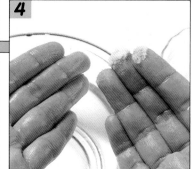

A SIMPLE WAY TO MAKE A RICE BALL AND VARIOUS SIMPLE TOOLS

Use plastic wrap.
❶ Spread plastic wrap and sprinkle salt over.
❷ Pick up four corners of the wrap, bring them together and wrap up the rice.
❸ Shape the rice ball as usual.

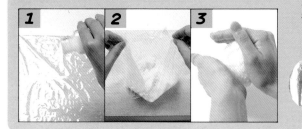

Plastic moulds

Heart, star, animals, etc.

Wooden press

Wet the press with water. Fill in cooked rice. Press from above and take out. An oval-shaped press is also available.

Packing container
Fill cooked rice in the container. Cover with a lid. A triangle rice ball will result.

Metal moulds
Each mould has a capacity of a bowl of cooked rice.

WELL-FORMED ONIGIRI

Triangle

Make a ball of rice. Cup one hand to hold the rice. Bend your other hand at the knuckles, and press the rice to form a triangle. Turn and repeat until it forms a regular triangle.

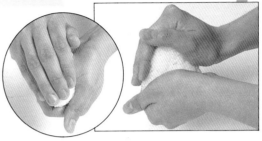

Barrel-shaped

Make a ball of rice. Cup one hand to hold the rice. Cupping your other hand, press both ends of the barrel while turning and rolling it into shape.

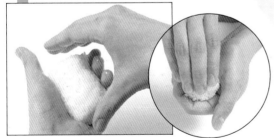

NORI SEAWEED AND SESAME SEEDS

To wrap in nori

Wrap the nori after the rice is cooled. If you wrap it while the rice is warm, it becomes soggy. But when covering the whole rice ball, wrap it up while the rice is warm so that the nori may stick to the rice ball.

To coat with sesame seeds

To coat the rice ball with sesame seeds, aonori or yukari, cover it while the rice is warm. When the rice is cooled, it becomes difficult to coat it well.

RICE MIXED WITH A VARIETY OF INGREDIENTS

TSUKUDANI

Ingredients (4 servings)
- **3** cups rice
- **2/3** cups tsukudani of shijimi
- **1** carrot
- **3** Tbsp sake

Tsukudani of shijimi is fresh-water clams (corbicula) cooked in sweetened soy sauce.

Method: ❶ Pare the carrot and cut into 1/8" (5 mm) cubes.

❷ Wash the rice. Cover with water plus 10% more sake than the quantity of rice.

❸ Mix in the tsukudani and carrot and cook as usual. Make rice balls without using salt.

Note: Adjust the amount of the tsukudani according to the taste. You may add the tsukudani of kombu (kelp) or broken-up pickled ume flesh.

COWPEAS

Ingredients (4 servings)
- **3** cups rice
- **1/3** cup cowpeas
- **1** Tbsp salt

Simple and easy rice with red beans.

Method: ❶ Wash cowpeas and discard hardened and worm-eaten ones. Boil in plenty of water and discard the water. Repeat this two or three times to remove the bitter taste.

❷ Simmer over low heat until tender. Let stand in the liquid until cooled.

❸ Add the liquid to the rice and cover with water until the whole amount is 10% more than the quantity of the rice. Let stand for about 30 minutes until rice is colored.

❹ Add cowpeas and cook as usual. When cooked, add salt and mix well. Make rice balls without using salt.

MUSHROOMS

Ingredients (4 servings)
- **3** cups rice
- **1** pack shimeji mushrooms
- **2** packs enokidake mushrooms
- **1** pack shiitake mushrooms
- Ⓐ
  - **2** Tbsp soy sauce
  - **2** Tbsp sake
  - **1** Tbsp mirin
  - **1 1/2** tsp salt

Enjoy the flavor of mushrooms.

Method: ❶ Remove the stems of mushrooms. Break up shimeji and enokidake and cut shiitake into thin slices. Don't wash them in water. Remove the dirt with a wet kitchen towel.

❷ Wash the rice and add Ⓐ. Cover with water a little less than 10% the amount of rice.

❸ Add the mushrooms and mix. Cook the rice as usual.

❹ Make rice balls without using salt.

CHICKEN

Ingredients (4 servings)

3 cups rice
2 chicken thighs
Ⓐ for broth
{ **4** Tbsp sugar
1/3 cup soy sauce
1/4 cup sake
1/2 tsp ginger juice
3 1/2 oz (100 g) string beans
3 Tbsp sake

Seasoned with chicken broth.

Method: ❶ Cut the chicken meat into 1/2" (1.5 cm) pieces.

❷ Boil Ⓐ in a pot and add the chicken. Boil down until the liquid thickens. Add the ginger juice.

❸ Boil the string beans in salted water. Cut into diagonal slices.

❹ Wash the rice and add the sake. Cover with 10% more water than the quantity of the rice. Cook as usual.

❺ Add the chicken together with the liquid to the cooked rice. Make rice balls without using salt.

SHISO CHIRIMEN

Ingredients (4 servings)

3 cups rice
Some shiso chirimen
20 pieces aojiso (green shiso leaves)
1/3 cup toasted sesame seeds
3 Tbsp sake

Shiso chirimen is dried young sardines mixed with shredded shiso (beefsteak plant) leaves.

Method: ❶ Wash the rice. Add the sake and cover with 10% more water than the quantity of rice. Cook as usual.

❷ Mix in the shiso chirimen, sesame seeds, aojiso (green shiso leaves) cut into julienne strips. Make rice balls without using salt.

Note: Instead of the shiso chirimen, you may mix in sansho (prickly ash) chirimen or furikake (condiment for sprinkling over rice).

CHRYSANTHEMUMS AND GINKGO NUTS

Ingredients (4 servings)

3 cups rice
10 edible chrysanthemums
20~30 ginkgo nuts
10~15 shelled walnuts
1 Tbsp salt
3 Tbsp sake

Colorful onigiri.

Method: ❶ Pick the petals from the chrysanthemums and parboil in a little vinegared water. Transfer immediately to cold water. Drain and squeeze liquid out.

❷ Shell the ginkgo nuts and boil in water. Skin and cut into slices. Chop the walnuts.

❸ Wash the rice. Add the sake and cover with 10% more water than the quantity of the rice. Cook as usual.

❹ Mix in the ingredients and salt. Make rice balls.

OMELET WITH MITSUBA & ENOKI

Ingredients (4 servings)

4 eggs	**2** tsp sugar
1/2 bunch mitsuba (honewort)	**1/2** tsp salt
1/2 pack enokidake mushrooms	Dash salad oil

Features the crisp enoki and flavor of mitsuba.

Method: ❶ Cut away root clusters of mushroom's and cut together with mitsuba into pieces.

❷ Beat eggs. Add the sugar and salt and mix well. Oil a pan and make an omelet.

VEGETABLES DRESSED WITH MAYONNAISE

Ingredients (4 servings)

1 small carrot	**1/2** broccoli
4 turnips	Mayonnaise

Method: ❶ Cut the carrot into round slices and the turnips into 6 or 8 portions. Divide the florets of the broccoli. ❷ Add the carrot, turnips, broccoli to boiling water in this order giving each time before adding the next. Cook until tender and then transfer to cold water. Drain well and dress with the mayonnaise.

MARINATED SALMON

Ingredients (4 servings)

4 fillets salmon	Sauce
Dash cornstarch	**1/2** naganegi (Japanese bunching onion)
Oil for deep-frying	**1** red chili pepper
	1/2 Tbsp sugar
	1/2 Tbsp vinegar
	2 Tbsp soy sauce
	2 Tbsp sake or water

A little stronger taste is recommended for use in lunch boxes.

Method: ❶ Remove seeds from the chili pepper. Cut the naganegi and chili pepper into thin round slices. Mix in the sauce mixture and bring to a boil.

❷ Cut salmon fillets diagonally and dust with the cornstarch. Preheat the oil to 340°F (170°C) and deep-fry until crispy.

❸ Marinate in the sauce and let stand until cooled.

CHICKEN AND BOILED EGGS FLAVORED WITH SOY SAUCE

Ingredients (4 servings)

2 filets chicken thighs
2 boiled eggs
1 clove ginger, sliced
Ⓐ { 2 Tbsp sugar
3~4 Tbsp soy sauce
3 Tbsp sake
1 Tbsp soy sauce
2 Tbsp salad oil

Method: ❶ Cut the chicken into bite-sized pieces. Sauté in oil until light brown. ❷ Add the ginger slices, Ⓐ and 1/2 cup water. Boil down until the liquid is almost evaporated. Remove the chicken. ❸ Add the eggs, soy sauce and 1/2 cup water to the chicken broth, and simmer, rolling the eggs, until evenly colored. ❹ When the liquid has evaporated, add the chicken and mix well.

LEMON FLAVORED INSTANT PICKLES

Ingredients (4 servings)

7 oz (200 g) mix of cabbage, carrot, cucumber
Salt (1% of the amount of vegetables)
3 lemon slices

Method: ❶ Trim off stems of cabbage leaves and cut into pieces. Slice thinly the carrot and cucumber.

❷ Put the vegetables in a bowl and sprinkle salt over. Add lemon slices cut into a fan shape. Place a light stone weight on the whole. ❸ Let stand overnight. Lightly wring out water from the vegetables.

Note: When you are in a hurry, increase the salt to about 1.5%.

SATÉED SCALLOPS IN CHINESE-SYTLE

Ingredients (4 servings)

8 small fresh scallops
2 green peppers
1/2 naganegi (Japanese bunching onion)
1 clove each of garlic and ginger
1/2 red chili pepper
2 Tbsp sesame oil
3 Tbsp each of soy sauce and sake
1 1/2 Tbsp sugar

Method: ❶ Cut the scallops horizontally in half. Cut the pepper into coarse pieces. ❷ Mince the vegetables and cut the chili pepper into round thin slices. ❸ Heat 1 Tbsp oil in a pan. First, sauté the scallops and then the green peppers. Remove each from the pan. ❹ Add the rest of the oil, ② and seasonings and bring to a boil. Add the sautéed scallops and green peppers and mix well.

THE ORIGIN OF ONIGIRI

Onigiri, which literally means 'grasping,' is also called 'omusubi' (binding together). Both words are not old terms. The archaic word for onigiri is 'tonjiki.' The term appears in ' Murasaki Shikibu's Diary' of the Heian period (794-1185). In ancient times, tonjiki was customarily given to common people on the occasion of a court function, so it was considered as one of the humble foods. According to a book on ancient practices and usages at court, which was published in 1843 (Edo period), tonjiki seems to be a kind of barrel-shaped glutinous rice ball. The onigiri originally was a food which was served to subordinate workers or soldiers on guard.

JAPANESE REGIONAL ONIGIRI

Each part of Japan has its own unique onigiri characteristic of its region. Some are traditional styles of onigiri handed down from generation to generation and some are onigiri which make use of the special products of its district. There is great diversity. Here is a survey of them. Mark ◎ refers to the onigiri introduced in this book.

Kyushu region

Oni no tekoboshi (Fukuoka)
Whale onigiri (Nagasaki)
Chicken onigiri (Nagasaki)
Taro onigiri (Nagasaki)
◎ Wild plants onigiri (Ooita, p.25)
Shiitake onigiri (Ooita)
◎ Pumpkin onigiri (Okinawa, p.25)
Casa onigiri (Okinawa)
Taimo onigiri (Okinawa)

Chugoku region

Yuzu kiritanpo (Shimane)
Koutake onigiri (Hiroshima)
Wakame onigiri (Yamaguchi)
◎ Tea leaves onigiri
(Yamaguchi, p.25)

Kinki region

Mehari-zushi (Mie)
◎ Bamboo shoots sushi (Kyoto, p.24)
Fuki-tawara (Kyoto)
Nae-meshi (Kyoto)
Black soybeans onigiri (Hyogo)
Mehari-zushi (Nara)
◎ Mehari-zushi (Wakayama, p.24)

Shikoku region

◎ Wakame onigiri (Tokushima, p.25)
Sudachi onigiri (Tokushima)

Hokkaido region

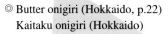

◎ Butter onigiri (Hokkaido, p.22)
  Kaitaku onigiri (Hokkaido)

Chubu region

  Chimaki (Niigata)
◎ Kenzan-yaki (Niigata, p.23)
  Hoba-meshi (Toyama)
  Hoba-meshi (Fukui)
◎ Hyakumanben (Yamanashi, p.23)
  Gohei-mochi (Nagano)
  Sugari gohan (Nagano)
◎ Gohei-mochi (Gifu, p.24)
◎ Kassen musubi (Aichi)
  Gohei mochi (Aichi)

Tohoku region

◎ Chrysanthemum flavor (Aomori, p.22)
◎ Rolled barley okowa onigiri (Iwate, p.22)
  Fuki onigiri (Iwate)
  Bakuro-meshi (Iwate)
  Walnuts in kaki leaf onigiri (Miyagi)
  Shiso & wakame onigiri (Miyagi)
  Damakko-mochi (Akita)
◎ Tanpo-mochi (Yamagata, p.23)
◎ Sasa-maki (Yamagata, p.22)
  Gomoku sasamaki (Fukushima)

Kanto region

  Yakimochi (Ibaraki)
  Bandai-mochi (Tochigi)
  Gomoku onigiri (Tochigi)
  Yude-mochi (Tochigi)
◎ Meshiyaki-mochi (Gunma, p.23)
  Kibi sekihan (Gunma)
  Cherry onigiri (Kanagawa)
  Gonan onigiri (Kanagawa)
  Chicken rice onigiri (Kanagawa)

BUTTER ONIGIRI

Hokkaido

A tasty onigiri grilled with butter, a special product of Hokkaido.

Ingredients & Method: ❶ Fill rice ball with tarako (salted pollack roe) or salmon.

❷ Melt butter (2 tsp for 4 rice balls) in a frying pan. Grill both sides of the rice ball over low heat. Coat with soy sauce and grill until brown.

CHRYSANTHEMUM FLAVOR

Aomori Prefecture

This onigiri originated from the fact that the feudal lord had brought edible chrysanthemums from Kyoto.

Ingredients & Method: ❶ Add a dash of vinegar to water and boil yellow chrysanthemums briefly. Boil fresh soybeans, skin and mince coarsely.

❷ Cut off root clusters of shimeji mushrooms. Add sake and stir-fry briefly.

❸ Add a dash of each soy sauce, sake and salt to rice and cook as usual. Mix the cooked rice with the ingredients. Make into rice balls of any shape.

ROLLED BARLEY OKOWA ONIGIRI

Iwate Prefecture

Rolled barley is easy to digest and does not sit heavy in the stomach, so it is favored by elderly people.

Ingredients & Method: ❶ The ratio of glutinous rice to barley is 10 to 1. Wash them separately. Soak the rice in water for 5 hours and the barely 1 hour.

❷ Wash salted bracken and wakame seaweed under running water. Cut them into small pieces.

❸ Mix the rice and barley and steam for 20 minutes. Mix in ② and steam further 15~20 minutes. Make rice balls.

SASA-MAKI

Yamagata Prefecture

This onigiri is symbolic to wish for young boys to grow up in good health.

Ingredients & Method: ❶ Wash glutinous rice and soak in water overnight. Drain and let stand for 1~2 hours before cooking.

❷ Wrap in 2 bamboo leaves (sasa) and tie with sedges.

❸ Cook slowly in water plus the clear part on the top of limewater for about 2 hours. Let stand for an hour until cooled to body temperature.

❹ Coat with molasses and soybean flour before eating.

TANPO-MOCHI

Yamagata Prefecture

Charcoal makers created this food to make use of leftover rice to eat between meals. To spend the long winter in this region, people
sit round the fire and enjoy chatting, eating this food.
Ingredients & Method: ❶ Cook rice rather firmly.
Mash the rice and knead. Put it on cedar skewers.
❷ Grill over charcoal until the surface dries. Coat with
kurumi-miso (see ① of Kenzan-yaki below) and grill
further turning around until brown.

MESHIYAKI-MOCHI

Gunma Prefecture

This snack is eaten by farmers when taking a break.
Ingredients & Method: ❶ Mince naganegi (Japanese bunching onion)
and aojiso (green shiso leaves). Sift flour with a dash of baking
soda added.
❷ Add miso, milk and ① to flour and the same quantity of cooked
rice. Knead the whole until it becomes a little harder than your
earlobe. Let stand for more than a half day.

❸ Heat a thick frying pan and fry
without using oil. When one side
is done, turn over and continue
frying covered with a lid.

HYAKUMANBEN

Yamanashi Prefecture

Hyakumanben is saying prayers a million times. In the Edo period this
onigiri was served when gathering to pray to Amitabha a million times.
Now it is made to wish for an easy delivery. Fill a small stone in about
1/3 of the onigiri and those who get them are said to have a baby boy.
Ingredients & Method: ❶ Soak adzuki beans in water for a half day.
Cook them until tender.
❷ Cook rice as usual and let in steam for a while. Add adzuki beans
and mix roughly. Smear salt on your palms and make rice balls with a
well-washed small stone in the middle. Shape the rice balls like a golf
ball.

KENZAN-YAKI

Niigata Prefecture

Kenzan is said to be the rice which is left after it was delivered to
the ruler as land tax.
Now this onigiri is made to celebrate the harvest of new rice.
Ingredients & Method: ❶ Grind walnuts in an earthenware
mortar. Add miso, sugar and sake and stir slowly over low
heat until sticky. This is called kurumi-miso.
❷ Cook rice a little firmer. Let it steam a little shorter than
usual and break it up.
❸ Make a rice ball into an oval shape and grill over charcoal. Coat
with ① and grill further until the surface dries and turns brown.

GOHEI-MOCHI
Gifu Prefecture

It looks like 'Gohei' (strips of white paper used in Shinto rituals), and hence its name. This is popular in mountainous districts in Gifu, Nagano and Aichi Prefectures.

Ingredients & Method: ❶ Grind cooked rice roughly in an earthenware mortar. Put it on skewers squeezing together with palms.

❷ Grill over charcoal until the surface dries. Coat with your favorite ingredients such as kurumi-miso (see p. 23) or peanut-miso. Continue grilling until it smells fragrant.

KASSEN-MUSUBI
Aichi Prefecture

Kassen means 'battle.' At the crucial battle of Nagashino in 1575, Tokugawa Ieyasu carried this musubi (rice balls). Takeda Katsuyori carried gohei-mochi.

Ingredients & Method: ❶ Spread aka-miso (dark-brown miso) into a flat oval shape. Grill both sides. Tear it and make small balls like golf balls.

❷ Place each miso ball in the center of hot cooked rice and make rice balls firmly.

❸ Toast both sides of the balls on a grid until the surface dries. Brush with tamari-joyu (rich soy sauce) and then toast again briefly until it smells fragrant.

BAMBOO SHOOTS SUSHI
Kyoto Prefecture

Sushi rice stuffed in cooked takenoko (bamboo shoots). This is served during shrine festivals.

Ingredients & Method: ❶ Cook boiled bamboo shoots and season lightly with dashi stock, soy sauce, and mirin. Remove bamboo joints.

❷ Cook bracken, shiitake mushrooms, carrot and abura-age (fried tofu) in the same way as above. Let stand until cooled.

❸ Make sushi rice with a little vinegar. Mix with drained ② and chopped joints of bamboo shoots. Stuff the mixture in the bamboo shoots and cut into bite-sized pieces.

MEHARI-ZUSHI
Wakayama Prefecture

The word 'mehari' means 'opening one's eyes wide.' One of these onigiri is made of about a cup of rice. The name of this giant onigiri comes from the fact that you open your mouth and eyes wide when eating.

Ingredients & Method: ❶ Chop pickled takana (leaf mustard) and mix roughly with cooked rice, dried bonito flakes, and toasted white sesame seeds .

❷ Spread takana leaves and place a rice ball on it. Wrap in the leaves.

TEA LEAVES ONIGIRI
Yamaguchi Prefecture

This onigiri was devised to make use of Takase-tea, a specialty of this district.

Ingredients & Method: ❶ Soak soy beans in water overnight. Chop up toasted peanuts.

❷ Place drained rice in a pot. Mix in ①, dashi stock, sake and salt. Place on heat.

❸ When it comes to a boil, add tea leaves (2~3 tsp for 3 cups of rice) and cook as usual. Let stand for 15 minutes after the heat is turned off. Make rice balls.

WAKAME ONIGIRI
Tokushima Prefecture

This onigiri was designed for wakame seaweed, a specialty of Tokushima. It carries the smell of the sea. Thin omelets garnish the onigiri.

Ingredients & Method: ❶ Mix cooked hot rice with chirimenjako (dried young sardines), and chopped wakame seaweed.

❷ Make rice balls into barrel shapes. Wrap in a thin omelet in place of the usual nori seaweed.

WILD PLANTS ONIGIRI
Ooita Prefecture

This onigiri is made on March 21 and September 21 at the festivals of the famous Buddhist priest, Kobo Daishi. Ingredients fried in oil make this onigiri tasty.

Ingredients & Method: ❶ Cut bracken, bamboo shoots, and reconstituted cloud ear mushrooms in bite-sized pieces. Sauté them in oil.

❷ Season the ingredients with sugar, light-colored soy sauce and salt. Mix with cooked glutinous rice. Make triangular rice balls.

PUMPKIN ONIGIRI
Okinawa Prefecture

Pumpkins have come to be cultivated in this district after World War II. The point of this onigiri is to use dashi stock in place of water and to cook with salad oil added.

Ingredients & Method: ❶ Remove seeds from the pumpkin and dice. Dice pork, carrot and kamaboko (boiled or steamed fish paste). Cut reconstituted dried shiitake mushrooms in strips.

❷ Add ①, dashi stock, a pinch of salt, salad oil (2 Tbsp for 3 cups of rice) to rice. Cook as usual. When done, add chopped negi (Japanese bunching onion) and make rice balls.

FANCY ONIGIRI

It is fun to make your own original rice balls. You can work out a variety of forms. These rice balls are suitable for snacks at tea time and parties.

WRAPPING ONIGIRI

Ingredients (4 servings)

- 1 cup scrambled eggs
- 1 red pepper
- 1/2 cup green peas
- 2 slices cheese
- 2 radish
- 2 pods okra
- 4 Tbsp ebisoboro (seasoned shrimp powder)
- 1 young cucumber
- 4 salted cherry blossoms
- 2 Tbsp aonori (green seaweed powder)
- 4 cups cooked rice

Make a golf ball-sized rice ball.

Arrange main colorful ingredients.

Cute onigiri with a variety of patterns.

Method: Make rice balls first. Sprinkle a dash of salt over plastic wrap. Place half the amount of usual onigiri on it. Wrap the rice and gather edges together tightly.

Scrambled Eggs, Pepper & Green Peas

❶ To make scrambled eggs: Beat 2 eggs, 1 egg yolk, 1 1/2 tsp sugar and a dash of salt. Cook over low heat, stirring continually with some chopsticks. Dice pepper into 1/8" (5 mm) cubes and boil with green peas for a short time.

❷ Make rice balls as shown in the photos.

Sprinkle with scrambled eggs or ebisoboro.

Put the onigiri on the ingredients softly.

Cheese, Radishes & Okra

❶ Cut cheese into strips and radishes into a fan shape. Rub okra with salt and cut into round thin slices.

❷ Place the ingredients on plastic wrap and twist as shown in the photos.

Ebisoboro & Cucumber

Place young cucumber slices on plastic wrap and sprinkle the ebisoboro over. Make rice balls as shown in the photos.

Cherry blossoms & Aonori

Rinse cherry blossoms in water to get rid of salt. Place them on plastic wrap and sprinkle the aonori over. Make rice balls as shown in the photos.

Bring the edges of wrap together firmly.

Twist the wrap tightly so that the ingredients stick to the rice.

THE NUTRITIONAL VALUE OF RICE

Rice is one of the world's most important food crops. In fact, half of the world's peoples eat rice as their staple food. Cooked rice looks beautiful and it is tasty. We never tire of eating it every day. It is becoming popular as a health food throughout the world.

In 3 1/2 oz (100 g) of polished rice, there is 2 3/5 oz (75.5 g) of carbohydrates (glucide). If chewed well, it tastes sweet, showing that it has a lot of glucide. This glucide is the source of our energy.

Although low in protein (6.8 g), its protein quality is good because it contains relatively high levels of the amino acid lysine. It is equal to the protein of beef, soybeans and milk. The quantity is 1.5 times as much as wheat flour.

Rice can be preserved for a long time. It is easy to cook and goes well with other dishes, which make up for the deficiency of nutrients of rice. Rice is an ideal food to keep good health.

● ONIGIRI IN ICE CREAM CONE ●

Ingredients (for 3 cones)

1 Tbsp shibazuke (assorted vegetables hashed and pickled in salt) Dash black sesame seeds	Some green leaves furikake (condiment for sprinkling over rice) 1 cherry tomato
1/2 cup scrambled eggs Some daikon sprouts	3 cup cooked rice 3 ice cream cones

Children will be pleased with the rice ball in a cone, because they can eat it like ice cream.

Method: ❶ Scrambled eggs: In a small pan beat together 1 egg, 1/2 egg yolk, 2/3 tsp sugar and a dash of salt. Cook, stirring with some chopsticks over low heat.

❷ When cooled, mix with one third of the cooked rice. Sprinkle a little salt over palms and shape the rice into a small ball to fit in the cone.

❸ Mix the furikake with one third of the cooked rice and the shibazuke with the other one third of the cooked rice. Make these rice balls without using salt in palms, because the pickles have enough salt.

❹ Top with daikon sprouts on the scrambled egg cone, cherry tomato on the furikake cone, and black sesame seeds on the shibazuke cone. Each cone is colorful.

● COOKIE-STYLE ONIGIRI ●

Ingredients (for 2 rice balls each)

1/2 slice cheese A bit of watercress	2 slices kamaboko (steamed fish-paste cake) 1 quail egg Dash black sesame seeds
1 Tbsp aonori (See. p.27) A bit of amazu-shoga (sweet-sour pickled ginger)	
1/2 slice ham A bit of cucumber	1~2 aojiso (green shiso leaves) Dash red pepper
1 Tbsp sakura-denbu (mashed and seasoned fish) A bit of parsley	1/2 slice cheese Dash pickled ume flesh 4 cups cooked rice

Cute bite-sized onigiri shaped with cookie cutters. Suitable for those who want to try a variety of tastes.

Method: ❶ Boil the quail egg in salted water. Shell and cut into thin slices. Chop the pepper and cut the ginger and cucumber into fine strips.

❷ Moisten cookie cutters with water. Fill the cooked rice in the cutter and press firmly with hands to make desired shapes.

❸ Top with the denbu and aonori by using a bamboo skewer. Cut the cheese and ham with the same cutter in the shapes of onigiri.

❹ Arrange the toppings as shown in photos.

● CANDY-STYLE ONIGIRI ●

Ingredients (4 servings)

1 Tbsp yukari (minced salted and dried shiso leaves)	Dash tororo-kombu (seaweed tangle flakes) 1" (2.5 cm) takuan (yellow pickled daikon)
1 Tbsp bonito furikake (flakes for sprinkling over rice)	1 Tbsp pickled green leaves, chopped 4 cups cooked rice

Mix the cooked rice with ingredients and wrap in sheets of cellophane paper like candies. It is exciting to open the paper, guessing what is inside.

Method: ❶ Chop the takuan and green leaves into fine pieces.

❷ Divide hot rice into 5 portions and mix with each ingredient.

❸ Wrap each rice in plastic wrap and make a rice ball, about the size of a golf ball. And wrap again in cellophane or pretty wrapping paper like a candy.

Note: This onigiri is convenient for on the go and suitable for hiking. You may also make a necklace with this onigiri.

● SANDWICH ONIGIRI ●

Ingredients (4 servings)

1 small can of corned beef
4~5 lettuce leaves

1 small can of tuna
2 pickles
1 tsp shoyu
1/3 tsp salt
Dash pepper
2 Tbsp mayonnaise

2 eggs
2 tsp curry powder
1/3 tsp salt
Dash pepper
2~3 Tbsp mayonnaise

6 cups cooked rice
1/2 tsp salt

Everyone will be amazed at this fantastic sandwich. Include this in one of your favorite recipes for your pleasure trip.

Method: ❶ Break up the corned beef into rough pieces. Wash the lettuce and drain.

❷ Drain oil off the tuna thoroughly and break up. Mince the pickles. Place the tuna and pickles in a bowl. Add the seasonings and mix well.

❸ Make hard-boiled eggs by boiling in salted water for 15 minutes. Shell and chop finely. Add the seasonings and mix until the mixture becomes pasty.

❹ Spread plastic wrap, two times larger than the box, in the lunch box. Spread 1 cup rice mixed with salt evenly (the quantity of rice depends on the size of the lunch box). Press the rice lightly with fingertips.

❺ Spread the fillings and press evenly with fingertips, leaving no space in the corners.

❻ Spread another 1 cup rice, leveling. Cover the rice with plastic wrap which sticks out of the lunch box. Place another wrap over.

❼ Put a light stone on ⑥ to get rid of air between rice layers. You may also press with a palm firmly.

❽ Remove the whole from the box and place on a board upside down. Let stand for a while so that the rice layers become uniform.

❾ Cut together with the plastic wrap into sandwich pieces and peel off the wrap. Cut nori seaweed into the same size as the pieces and stick to both sides. The nori makes it easy to eat by hand.

Place plastic wrap in the lunch box. Spread the rice sprinkled with salt.

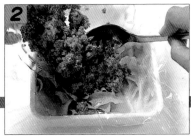

Arrange the fillings all over the rice.

Spread the rice again and even out with fingertips.

Turn upside down and let stand for a while to make the surface level.

Cut together with the wrap in a little larger size.

Stick the nori of the same size to both sides of the rice. It makes it easy to eat by hand.

FOLK CUSTOMS OF ONIGIRI

On New Year's Eve, twelve or thirteen rice balls (as many as the months) with each speared with a chopstick are offered on a winnow to a family Shinto or Buddhist altar.

They are called 'nidama-meshi' or 'mitama.' In some districts, rice balls or rice in a bowl are served at funerals, following the custom of eating the last supper with the deceased.

Ingredients (1 cake 8 1/2" (22 cm) across)

● Chirashi-zushi
2 cups sushi rice (p.48)
1 carrot

Ⓐ {
2 tsp sugar
Pinch salt
2 Tbsp sake
2 Tbsp water
}

2 abura-age
  (deep-fried tofu)
1/2 cup dashi stock
1 Tbsp sugar
1 tsp soy sauce
1/2 tsp salt
1 Tbsp sake

5~6 dried shiitake mushrooms
{
1 Tbsp sugar
2 tsp soy sauce
}

● Decorations
Scrambled eggs
{
3 eggs
2 egg yolks
2 Tbsp sugar
1/3 tsp salt
}

2/3 cups sakura-denbu
  (mashed and seasoned fish)
2 cucumbers
Some sprigs kinome
  (young leaves of prickly ash)

Chirashi-zushi is sushi rice scattered with a variety of colorful ingredients. This fancy sushi will attract a great deal of attention at a party.

Method: ❶ Cut the carrot into fine strips. Add Ⓐ and cook, stirring continually until tender.
❷ Dip the abura-age in hot water to remove excess oil and cut into strips. Cook in the dash stock and sake for 5 minutes. Add sugar and cook for another 5 minutes. Add shoyu and salt and simmer for 10 minutes until the liquid is reduced.

❸ Soak the shiitake mushrooms in water. Squeeze out water and cut into slices. Cover with the water in which the shiitake was soaked. Cook for 15 minutes and then add sugar and cook for another 5 minutes. Add soy sauce and simmer until the liquid is almost gone.
❹ Prepare 2 cups sushi rice as illustrated on p. 48. While the rice is still warm, mix in the cooled ingredients to make chirashi-zushi.
❺ Decorations: Beat eggs, yolks and seasonings in a saucepan to make scrambled eggs. Heat the pan and cook the mixture, stirring continually with some chopsticks until it crumbles. Cut cucumbers into 3 parts and slice each part lengthwise. Sprinkle 1/2 tsp salt over and let soften.
❻ Spread plastic wrap on the base of cake tin and arrange the scrambled eggs, denbu and cucumber slices (photos 2~3).
❼ Scatter the chirashi-zushi over (photo 4). Fold down the edges of cucumber slices toward the rice and cover the whole with plastic wrap. Put a weight and let the sushi rice settle (photo 5).

Mix warm sushi rice and cooled ingredients.

Place scrambled eggs and sakura-denbu alternately in stripes. Use thick paper to separate the eggs and denbu. Arrange with a bamboo skewer, if necessary.

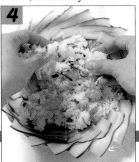

Place cucumber slices one upon another around the side.

Take care not to disturb the ingredients below.

Top with a flat plate and press under a weight.

ONIGIRI WRAPPED IN LETTUCE LEAVES

Ingredients (4 servings)

Niku-miso

- 7 oz (200 g) ground pork lean
- 2/3 naganegi (Japanese bunching onion)
- 2~3 Tbsp sweet miso
- 1~2 Tbsp sugar
- 3 Tbsp sake
- 2 Tbsp salad oil

4 cups cooked rice
1 head lettuce

Healthful onigiri designed to eat with plenty of vegetables. Use a miso which is not too salty.

Method: ❶ Chop the naganegi finely.

❷ Heat the oil in a pan over high heat and stir-fry the naganegi. When it smells fragrant add the ground pork immediately and continue stir-frying until crumbled.

❸ Sprinkle sake over and cover with a lid. Cook for 10 minutes over low heat. Periodically check and if the liquid is almost gone, add sake or water.

❹ Add the miso and sugar and simmer over low heat, stirring continually until thickened.

❺ Without using salt, make rice balls large enough to fit in the lettuce leaves. Place the rice ball on a lettuce leaf and top with the niku-miso. Wrap in the leaf before eating.

Note: The niku-miso can be stored in the refrigerator for a week. Since it goes well with vegetables, make extra.

CABBAGE ROLLS WITH ONIGIRI

Ingredients (4 servings)

3 cups cooked rice	Simmering Broth
⎧ 4 Tbsp dried bonito flakes	⎧ 4~5 cups dashi stock
⎨	⎨ 1 Tbsp soy sauce
⎩ 1 Tbsp soy sauce	⎨ 1 Tbsp sake
8 cabbage leaves	⎩ 1~1 1/2 tsp salt

In place of ground meat, stuff rice mixed with dried bonito flakes. Plain and simple Japanese-style flavor.

Method: ❶ Sprinkle the soy sauce over bonito flakes. Add the rice and mix well. Divide into 8 portions and make small rice balls without salt in palms.

❷ Pull off cabbage leaves one by one taking care not to tear. Put in a boiling water until softened.

❸ Drain in a colander and let cool. Pat dry on paper towels. Cut off the tough base of each leaf. (Don't cool the leaves in water, unless necessary. It will make them soggy.)

❹ Place one onigiri on each leaf and roll. Fold in one side and roll up and insert the other side into the hole of the roll to prevent from opening.

❺ Place 8 rolls in a pot side by side tightly with no space left in between. Cover with the simmering sauce to cook.

❻ Simmer for about 10 minutes and then add the sake and salt. Continue to simmer for another 10 minutes until the cabbage leaves are completely soft. Add the soy sauce before turning off the heat.

Fold in one side of the leaf and roll up.

Insert the other side into the hole.

Place rolls side by side and cover with the simmering sauce.

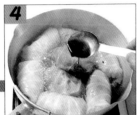

Cook until tender and add the soy sauce to finish.

FOUR VARIATIONS OF
INARI-ZUSHI

HOW TO SEASON ABURA-AGE

Ingredients

6~8 abura-age	**1** Tbsp mirin
4 Tbsp sugar	**2** Tbsp sake
3 Tbsp soy sauce	

Method: ❶ Put the abura-age side by side in a colander. Pour boiling water over to remove excess oil. To prepare lots of abura-age at a time, boil water in a pot and pass them through and drain in a colander.

❷ When cooled, squeeze water out and cut into the shape for inari-zushi. Slap the abura-age with hands or roll out with a wooden pestle on a cutting board to make it easy to open.

❸ Carefully open up the abura-age from cut side to make a pouch.

❹ Place in a pot and add the seasonings plus 1 cup water. Simmer over low heat, turning over occasionally.

❺ Simmer until the liquid is almost gone. Abura-age absorbs liquid like a sponge, so take care not to overcook or the surface dries.

❻ Squeeze the liquid out and fill the rice mixed with fillings. Make into the shape desired.

INARI-ZUSHI (Sushi rice in abura-age pouches)

Ingredients (for 4 pieces): 2 abura-age, **2** cups sushi rice (p. 48), tsukudani of konbu (kelp seaweed boiled in sweetened soy sauce)

Method: ❶ Cut the abura-age in half. Open and cook as shown in the photos.

❷ Prepare the sushi rice (p. 48). Add the tsukudani and run a spatula through the mixture in cutting motions.

❸ Squeeze liquid out of abura-age and turn it inside out. Stuff the abura-age pouch half full with sushi rice mixture. Make into a barrel shape.

SHINODA-MAKI (Sushi rice rolled in abura-age sheet)

Ingredients (for 2 rolls): 2 abura-age, **3** cups sushi rice (p. 48), amazu-shoga (sweet-sour pickled ginger), scallion

Method: ❶ Cut three sides of abura-age and open. Cook as shown in the photos.

❷ Cut the amazu-shoga into strips and the scallion into thin round slices (see photos). Mix them with the sushi rice

❸ Squeeze the liquid out and spread on a flat surface. Place the rice mixture ② on the abura-age. Roll in the shape of a cylinder like nori-maki. Cut into pieces.

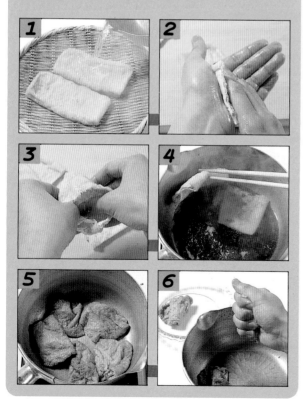

INARI-ZUSHI

SHINODA-MAKI

Scallion slices

Amazu-shoga strips

TRIANGLE INARI

Ingredients (for 4 pieces): 2 abura-age, **3** cups sushi rice (p. 48), **3~4** fresh shiitake mushrooms, dash toasted sesame seeds

Method: ❶ Cut one shorter side of abura-age and open. Cook as shown in the photos.
❷ Remove the stems of the shiitake and grill. Cut into thin strips. Prepare the sushi rice (p. 48) and mix with the shiitake strips.
❸ Squeeze the liquid out of the abura-age. Stuff with the rice mixture and fold the open end inside to close. Cut in half diagonally into triangles. Sprinkle with the sesame seeds.

Tsukudani

Shiitake mushrooms

CHAKIN INARI (Sushi rice wrapped in abura-age bag)

Ingredients (4 pieces): 4 abura-age, **2** cups sushi rice (p.48), **5** aojiso (green shiso) leaves, toasted sesame seeds, **4** stalks mitsuba (honewort)

Method: ❶ Cut the abura-age into 3/4 lengthwise and open. Chop the remaining 1/4 into pieces for fillings. Cook together as shown in the photos.
❷ Prepare the sushi rice (p.48). Mix with the aojiso cut into julienne strips, cooked abura-age pieces and sesame seeds.
❸ Squeeze the liquid out of the abura-age. Stuff with the rice mixture and tie the opening with boiled mitsuba.

VARIOUS FILLINGS

You may add carrots, shiitake mushrooms, and lotus roots as in chirashi-zushi. Shredded citron peels will also be good for fillings. In Osaka, hemp seeds are often used.

TRIANGLE INARI

CHAKIN INARI

Aojiso

Sesame seeds

COOKED ONIGIRI

This section presents ideas of cooking onigiri, such as savory toasted onigiri and crisp deep-fried onigiri.

TOASTING

Toasted onigiri is most popular among cooked onigiri. The savory smell of soy sauce and butter will fascinate you.

Enjoy a variety of tastes by using a grill, frying pan and oven toaster.

TOASTED ONIGIRI WITH SOY SAUCE

1

Regular   Toasting

The first point in making a toasted onigiri is to squeeze the rice more firmly than usual.

2

To prevent the rice from sticking to the grill, brush the grill with salad oil and heat it over a high heat until it turns red.

3

Toast rice balls some distance above the fire until they separate from the grill. If you remove too early, the onigiri will break up as shown in the photo.

4

When the front and back are done, toast the three sides until golden brown.

5

Brush the whole with shoyu and toast again lightly until the surface is dried.

PACKING OF ONIGIRI

Onigiri is an emergency food for evacuation and it is distributed after fires or when struck by earthquakes or typhoons. It is often carried as a handy lunch for a trip, because it is not bulky and it used to be wrapped in a disposable bamboo sheath or a paper-thin sheet of wood.

TOASTED ONIGIRI WITH MISO

Ingredients & Method: ❶ Make a flat rice ball and toast as shown in the left photo.
❷ Do not use salty miso. Combine with a little mirin as desired.
❸ Spread the miso over the surface thinly with fingers. Toast lightly until the miso is dried.

ON A GRILL

TOASTED ONIGIRI WITH CHEESE

IN A TOASTER OVEN

Ingredients & Method: ❶ Mix the rice with ketchup, chopped parsley and whole corn. Make an oval rice ball and top with cheese. (If it is difficult to make a ball, use plastic wrap.)
❷ Cook in a toaster oven until the cheese melts. Top with ketchup.

PICCATA ONIGIRI

Ingredients & Method: ❶ Beat 2 eggs for 4 rice balls. Combine with salt and pepper and 2~3 stalks chopped scallion.
❷ Make a flat rice ball. Dip in the egg mixture ①. Heat oil in a frying pan and cook.
❸ When both sides are done, dip again in the egg mixture and continue cooking until the mixture is gone.

IN A FRYING PAN

SMALL ONIGIRI WITH WALNUT MISO

ON A GRILL

Ingredients & Method: ❶ Ground 1 3/4 oz (50 g) walnuts. Combine with 1~2 Tbsp miso, 3~5 Tbsp sugar and 2~3 Tbsp sake. Cook over low heat, stirring until thickening.
❷ Make small rice balls and thread on skewers. Toast without any seasoning.
❸ Paste the miso over and dry over the fire, holding the skewer by hand.

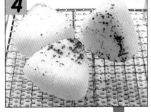

TOASTING

IN A TOASTER OVEN

FRIED ONIGIRI

Ingredients (4 servings)
4 cups cooked rice
Butter, sugar and soy sauce

Method: ❶ Divide the rice into 8 portions. Make small flat balls without using salt in palms.

TOASTED ONIGIRI WITH MAYONNAISE

Ingredients (4 servings)
3 cups cooked rice
4~5 ham slices
1 stalk celery
Mayonnaise
Dash salt and pepper
Cherry tomato
Watercress

Hot onigiri, which is good for cold midnight snacks.

Method: ❶ Cut the ham into fine pieces. Peel and chop the celery.
❷ Mix the hot rice with the ham, celery, salt and pepper. Make flat round rice balls.
❸ Make a ring of mayonnaise on top. Place the rice balls on a lightly oiled tin foil.
❹ Cook in a toaster oven until the mayonnaise is browned. Garnish with tomatoes and watercress.

WITH BUTTER

❷ Melt the butter in a frying pan. Fry the rice balls until both sides are lightly browned. Do not use too much butter, or the rice balls will crumble. About 2 tsp butter is appropriate for 4 balls, although the amount depends on the size of a frying pan.

❸ Pour the sugar and soy sauce over the hot rice balls as desired before serving.

IN A FRYING PAN

ON A GRILL

TOASTED ONIGIRI WITH GREEN TEA

Ingredients (4 servings)

4 cups cooked rice
Miso
Dash mirin (optional)
Dried bonito flakes
1 clove ginger
2~3 stalks scallion

Savor the plain taste by breaking up the rice balls. Instead of the miso, you may use soy sauce, and if you prefer a strong taste use dashi stock or soup in place of the green tea.

Method: ❶ Make toasted onigiri as shown on p. 39. Spread the miso and toast until it smells savory.

❷ Cut the ginger into julienne strips and the scallion into round thin slices.

❸ Put the onigiri in a bowl. Top with the ginger, scallion and dried bonito flakes. Pour hot green tea over.

DEEP-FRYING

RICE CROQUETTES

Ingredients (4 servings)

4 cups cooked rice
{ Parsley
{ 1/3 tsp salt
{ Dash pepper
2 wieners
2 4/5 oz (80g) cheese

Batter
{ Flour
{ 1 beaten egg
{ Bread crumbs
Oil for deep-frying

Cute snack onigiri.

Method: ❶ Cut one wiener into 4 equal portions. Dice the cheese in cubes.

❷ Mince the parsley and mix in the rice with salt and pepper.

❸ Stuff either wiener or cheese in the center of 16 golf-ball sized rice balls.

❹ Dredge each ball with flour, dip into the beaten egg and roll in bread crumbs. Heat the oil to 325 F (170°C) and deep-fry the balls until golden brown.

❺ Drain well. Serve hot as is or top with ketchup as desired.

SHAPES OF ONIGIRI

Rice balls have a variety of shapes — round, triangle and barrel. It is said that they stand for our sincerity and symbolize our heart, lung and kidney. Onigiri, like rice cakes, is easy to shape as desired and so was often used as a votive offering. The onigiri given to attendants in the Heian Period had a barrel shape.

DEEP-FRIED RICE GYOZA

Ingredients (4 servings)

1 cup cooked rice	(A) { 2 tsp soy sauce
12 gyoza skins (store-bought)	{ 1 tsp sake
4~5 oz (100~150 g) ground pork	1/3 tsp salt
1 stalk naganegi	Dash pepper
(Japanese bunching onion)	Radish with leaves
1 clove ginger	Oil for deep-frying
1 Tbsp sesame seed oil	

Method: ❶ Chop the naganegi and ginger finely. Heat the sesame oil in a frying pan and stir-fry until it smells nutty. Add the ground pork and season with salt and pepper.

❷ Mix the rice with ① and Ⓐ. Place the rice mixture on the gyoza skins. Fold them by pressing the edge firmly to let out the air.

❸ Preheat the oil to 350 F (180°C) and deep-fry until golden brown. Garnish with the radish.

DEEP-FRIED SESAME DUMPLINGS

Ingredients (4 servings)

3 cups cooked rice	1/2 cup rinsed white
5 1/4 oz (150 g) an	sesame seeds
(sweet red-bean paste; store-bought)	Oil for deep-frying

A kind of savory cake with an in the middle and covered with sesame seeds.

Method: ❶ Mash the rice with a wooden pestle until it becomes slightly sticky (photo 1). If you do not mash, the oil will penetrate between grains and the balls will fall apart.

❷ When the rice becomes sticky, make it into a large ball and press and knead it with force. Divide the rice into 12 small balls.

❸ Divide the an into 12 balls and stuff each into a rice ball (photo 2). Roll them in the sesame seeds to cover.

❹ Preheat the oil to 320 F (160°C) and deep-fry until it smells done.

Ingredients (4 servings)

4 cups glutinous rice	1 naganegi
4 Tbsp dried small shrimp	(Japanese bunching onion)
4–5 dried shiitake mushrooms	7 Tbsp salad oil
7 oz (200 g) roast pork	1/4 cup sake
5 1/4 oz (150 g) boiled	2 Tbsp sugar
bamboo shoots	4 Tbsp soy sauce

CHINESE-STYLE CHIMAKI

Chimaki is cooked glutinous rice wrapped in bamboo sheaths. This recipe uses tin foil in place of bamboo leaves for home cooking.

Method: ❶ Wash the glutinous rice and soak in water overnight. Drain in a colander for 1~2 hours.

❷ Soak the shiitake mushrooms and small shrimp in tepid water. Drain and chop coarsely. Reserve the water in which they are soaked.

❸ Cut the roast pork and bamboo shoots into 3/8" (1 cm) cubes. Chop the naganegi into round slices 1/8" (5 mm) wide.

❹ Heat 3 Tbsp salad oil in a wok and stir-fry the naganegi briefly. When it smells fragrant, add the roast pork, bamboo shoots, shrimp and shiitake mushrooms and stir-fry.

❺ Add the rest of the oil and the glutinous rice. Continue to stir-fry until the rice absorbs the oil and looks clear.

❻ Add water to that from shiitake and shrimps for a total of 3 1/2 cups and add the sake. Pour the liquid on the rice at intervals, 2 to 3 times. Meanwhile add the sugar and soy sauce.

❼ When the liquid is gone and the rice is done, turn off the heat.

❽ Divide into 12 portions and wrap each with tin foil and mold into shape. Place in a prepared steamer and steam for 20~30 minutes.

When the naganegi becomes fragrant, stir-fry the remaining ingredients.

Add the drained glutinous rice and stir-fry until it looks clear.

Add liquid at intervals, several times.

Add seasonings and continue to cook until the rice is done.

Ingredients (4 servings)

3 cups cooked rice	**4** sausages
1 cup flour	**1** large can boiled
1/2 small cabbage	tomatoes
1 onion	**2** bouillon cubes
1 large carrot	Parsley, minced
1 stalk large celery	Pinch salt and pepper

RICE DUMPLINGS

Shape the dumplings smaller so that they are well seasoned.

Method: ❶ Quarter the onion and cabbage together with cores. Peel the celery and cut into 4 portions. Cut the carrot into 3 crosswise and then cut the thick part into 4 and the thin part in half. Use fresh sausages, if available.

❷ Place 4 cups water and bouillon cubes in a thick saucepan. Cook the vegetables for about 30 minutes, adding the carrot, onion, celery and cabbage in this order according to the hardness. Meanwhile add the tomatoes.

❸ Combine the cooked rice and flour to make dumplings. At first they remain separate, but if you knead them with force, they become a lump of dough because of the moisture of the rice.

❹ Shape the dough into small balls like golf balls. Drop into plenty of boiling water. When they come up to the surface, remove them to the soup of ②.

❺ Add the sausages and simmer for 10 minutes. Season with the salt and pepper to taste. Sprinkle with the minced parsley to serve.

1 Add the flour to the rice and knead with force.

2 Knead well and make a lump of dough.

3 Shape balls the size of golf balls.

4 Drop in boiling water and boil until the balls come to the surface.

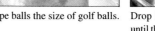

FANCY MAKI-ZUSHI

Maki-zushi or rolled sushi is made by rolling all of the ingredients in nori seaweed with the aid of a bamboo mat and cutting the rolls into serving pieces. Here are examples of modern variations of traditional designs in mind.

POINTS FOR SUCCESSFUL FANCY MAKI-ZUSHI

SUSHI RICE Cook more than 3 cups of rice for successful sushi rice.

● TO MAKE SUSHI RICE

Traditionally, a strip of kelp is added to the rice, but the Mizuno-method does not use kelp. Try either way, the Mizuno-method or the traditional method as desired.

Mizuno-method

Ingredients:

3 cups rice	3 1/3 cups water

Method: Wash the rice and drain in a colander for 1 hour. Add water and cook as usual. Turn off the heat and let stand for 7~8 minutes.

Traditional method

Ingredients:

3 cups rice	4 inches (10 cm) kelp
3 1/3 cups water + 2 Tbsp sake	

Method: Wash the rice and drain in a colander for 1 hour. Place the rice in a rice cooker. Add rice, water plus sake and kelp wiped clean with a wet dish towel. When it comes to a boil, remove the kelp. Cook as usual. Turn off the heat and let stand for 7~8 minutes.

● VINEGAR SEASONING

Ingredients:

4 Tbsp vinegar	1/2~1 tsp salt
2 Tbsp sugar	

Method: Dissolve sugar and salt in vinegar over low heat. Heat enough just to facilitate the dissolving process. The quantity of salt varies according to the kind of sushi prepared— 1/2 tsp for pickled fillings and 1 tsp for others.

1 After wetting a wooden tub, empty the cooked rice into it. Pour the vinegar seasoning over.

2 Run a spatula in slicing motions to separate the grains and mix thoroughly with the vinegar seasoning.

3 Spread the rice and fan to cool until the rice reaches room temperature.

4 Cover the tub with a wet towel until you are ready to use the rice.

KANPYO (Dried Gourd Strips)

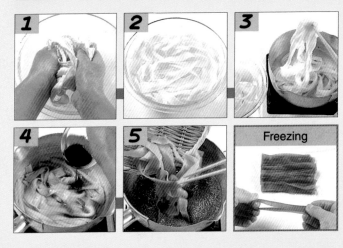

Freezing

Ingredients: 1 3/4 oz (50 g) kanpyo, 2 oz (60 g) sugar 1/2 cup soy sauce, 1/4 cup mirin

Method: ❶ Moisten the kanpyo with water and rub well with salt.

❷ Wash the salt away and soften by soaking in water.

❸ Cook until a little tender and then plunge into cold water immediately.

❹ Cut into the same length as nori seaweed (8 1/4" (21 cm)). Cover with water. Add the seasonings and cook until soft.

❺ Remove the kanpyo. Taste the kanpyo and season as desired. Simmer the liquid until reduced. Return the kanpyo and mix with the liquid. When freezing, fold in two and keep it in layers.

THE SIZE OF NORI

The surface of nori seaweed is glossy. On a makisu (bamboo mat), the nori is placed shiny-side down. A half sheet of nori means the sheet cut in half lengthwise.

Length: 8 1/4" (21 cm)
Width: 7" (18 cm)

1/2 sheet ... 3 1/2" (9 cm) wide
1/3 sheet ... 2 1/2" (6 cm) wide
1/4 sheet ... 1 1/2" (4.5 cm) wide
2/3 sheet ... 4 3/4" (12 cm) wide

UTENSILS

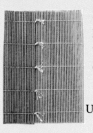

◊ **Makisu (Bamboo mat)**
Made of slender strips of bamboo woven together with cotton string. Select a larger one.

Scissors ◊
Used to cut the nori.

Cooking chopsticks ◊

Used to make grooves in the sushi rice. If you mark them with a graded scale, they are useful in measuring the length of the nori.

HOW TO ROLL AND CUT

1 For fancy maki-zushi, hold the makisu lengthwise.

The method is different from that of usual maki-zushi. Holding the makisu with both hands, tuck in towards the center alternately from both sides.

2 The quantity of rice determines the thickness.

At first spread the rice thinly. Do not place too much rice, or it will become difficult to roll up.

3 For hoso-maki (thin roll), place the nori horizontally.

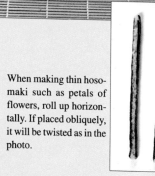

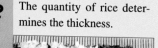

When making thin hoso-maki such as petals of flowers, roll up horizontally. If placed obliquely, it will be twisted as in the photo.

4 The edge of nori is put together one upon another.

Nori: Stick the two edges of nori one upon another where they come together. Thin egg omelet: Fill in a little extra rice so that the edges of omelet stick together.

5 Use 1/2 sheet of nori to make a variety of patterns.

In making various patterns, cut the nori sheet in half lengthwise. Use a little more rice than the usual quantity (1/2 of one roll).

6 Cut into 8 portions.

First, cut the roll in half with a sharp, wet knife, and then each of the halves in half, and so on until you obtain 8 equal pieces.

BASIC FANCY MAKI-ZUSHI

Enjoy various patterns of the finished pieces.

TURBAN SHELL

Ingredients (for 1 roll)
3 oz (80 g) chopped
   sea eel
1~2 pickled pokeweed
2 1/2 cup sushi rice (p.48)
2 1/2 sheets nori seaweed

Preparation of fillings
Chop one sea eel into 1/4" (7 mm) wide pieces and cut the pokeweed to the same length as the nori (8 1/4" (21 cm)).

1

Spread the rice thinly on 1/2 sheet of nori, leaving 5/8" (1.5 cm) open on both ends. Place the pokeweed in the center.

2

Make a hoso-maki by rolling up the rice with both hands and letting the ends of nori meet one upon another.

3

Spread the rice thinly on 1 sheet of nori, leaving 3/4" (2 cm) open on both ends. Make 5 grooves with a chopstick at equal intervals.

4

Press 1 sheet of nori into each groove, starting from 3/4" (2 cm) from the right side. Cut off the nori sticking out on the left side.

5

Align the chopped sea eel in each groove.

6

Spread the rice thinly, leaving 3/8" (1 cm) open on both ends. Place the hoso-maki in the center so that the seam of the nori comes to the top.

7

Hold each end of nori with thumbs and bring the whole together, pressing inward to make a cylinder.

8
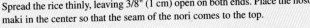
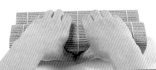
Hold the bamboo mat with the left hand. Add more rice in the space and fold over with the nori. Put the seam of the nori down and arrange the shape.

TULIP

Ingredients (for 1 roll)
- **1** wiener
- **2 3/4"** (7 cm) cooked carrot
- **2 3/4"** (7 cm) omelet
- **1** cucumber
- **2 1/2** cups sushi rice (p.48)
- **2** sheets nori seaweed

Preparation of fillings

Make a thin omelet and roll up in the shape of a stick while hot. Place on a bamboo mat laying a chopstick in the center and roll up as shown in the photo. Cook the carrot with sugar. Cut the carrot and wiener in the shape of flowers. Rub the cucumber with salt and cut in half lengthwise.

1
Spread the rice thinly on 1 sheet of nori, leaving 3/4" (2 cm) open on either side of the nori. Make two mounds of rice, 1/2" (1.5 cm) wide and 3/4" (2 cm) high, leaving a space for flower fillings between them.

2
Place the fillings with the cuts down. Bring the rice mounds together around the fillings, higher than the fillings.

3
Cut 1 1/8" (3 cm) off 1 sheet of nori and fold in half. Place it in the center of the fillings for stems and leaves.

4
Pinch the tops of the nori over the rice mounds. The nori between the top and the fillings makes the stems of flowers. Take care not to press the nori of either side of the rice too hard.

5
Place the cucumbers on both sides of the ridge of nori and fold over the nori and cover them. This accents the parts of leaves.

6
Hold both sides of the bamboo mat with hands and push inwards lightly to bring the whole together into a round shape.

7
Hold the bamboo mat with the left hand and spread the rice thinly over the cucumbers to cover completely.

8
Press each side alternately and bring the ends of nori together one upon another. Shape and arrange the whole.

DANDELION

Ingredients (for 1 roll)

1 egg, shredded thin omelet
1~2 pickled pokeweed
2 pickled nozawana (turnip greens)
2 1/2 cups sushi rice (p. 48)
2 sheets of nori seaweed

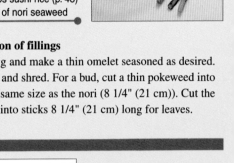

Preparation of fillings

Beat an egg and make a thin omelet seasoned as desired. Let it cool and shred. For a bud, cut a thin pokeweed into length the same size as the nori (8 1/4" (21 cm)). Cut the nozawana into sticks 8 1/4" (21 cm) long for leaves.

1

Spread the rice thinly on 1 sheet of nori, leaving 3/4" (2 cm) open on both ends. Place the shredded omelet on the rice, 2 1/2" (6 cm) from the left side of the nori.

2

Cut another nori into a strip, 3/4" (2 cm) wide, and place it on the omelet.

3

Add the rice on either side of the omelet and make two mounds of rice, 1/2" (1.5) cm wide and 3/4" (2 cm) high. On the right side, make another mound of rice in the center of the rice.

4

Fold the remaining nori, after the strip has been cut off, in half and place it on the center mound. Push it into the grooves on either side with a chopstick as shown.

5

Place the pokeweed in the groove on the right side, and the nozawana on the outside of either mounds.

6

Fold inward both ends of the upper nori and cover the nozawana.

7

Hold the bamboo mat with both hands and press lightly toward the center and roll up.

8

Add the rice thinly to fill in the space. Bring the ends of nori together and make into a round shape.

SASANQUA

Ingredients (for 1 roll)

1 Tbsp sakura-denbu
  (mashed and seasoned fish)
1~2 pickled pokeweeds
1 Tbsp chopped vinegared ginger
2 pickled nozawana (turnip greens)
2 1/2 cups sushi rice (P. 48)
3 sheets of nori seaweed

Preparation of fillings

Mix a handful of rice and sakura-denbu for pink petals. Cut a thin pokeweed into length the same size of the nori (8 1/4" (21 cm)). Select two kinds of nozawana, thin and thick. Cut them into length the same size as the nori. Use a thin nozawana for a bud and a thick one for leaves.

1

Cut 1 sheet of nori into 6 equal portions (one strip is 1 1/8" (3 cm) wide). Spread the nori parallel to the bamboo mat. Place the rice and denbu mixture in the center. Move both sides of the bamboo mat, pressing alternately and roll up 5 thin rolls as shown. It is unnecessary for the nori to overlap in this case.

2

Petal

Center of a flower

Roll up the pokeweed with 1/4 sheet of nori completely.

3

Set the bamboo mat as shown and arrange thin rolls with the pokeweed in the center.

4

Spread the rice thinly on 1 sheet of nori, leaving 3/4" (2 cm) open on both ends. Place the flowers at 2 1/2" (6 cm) from the left end of the nori. Make mounds of rice, one on the right side of the flowers and the other at 2 1/2" (6 cm) from the right side of the nori.

5

Cover the right side with the remaining nori (3/4 sheet after 1/4 cut off). Push in the groove with a chopstick.

6

Pinch the nori and rice together and raise them like a ridge.

7

Put the chopped ginger in the groove and place thin nozawana on it and thick one on the right.

8

Fold the nori over and cover the nozawana on the right side of the mound.

9

Lightly press from both sides. Spread the rice thinly. Bring the nori together and make the ends meet. Shape into a cylinder.

FANCY MAKI-ZUSHI CALENDAR

JAN WAVE PATTERNS

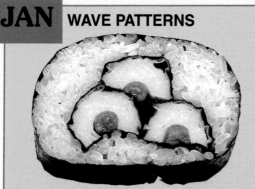

Cut chikuwa (steamed fish-paste tube) in half lengthwise. Stuff with stems of pickled turnip greens. Roll it in 1/2 sheet nori. (Place grated horseradish for adults.) Mix rice with flesh of ume as desired and roll it together with chikuwa.

APR CHERRY BLOSSOMS

See Sasanqua on p. 53 for rolling.

Mix rice with denbu (mashed and seasoned fish) for petals and roll in 1/4 sheet of nori. Place rice mixed with yukari (minced salted and dried shiso leaves) between petals. Make flower center and bud with pokeweed and stem and calyx with turnip greens.

FEB WINTER CAMELLIA

See Sasanqua on p. 53 for rolling.

Mix rice with grilled pollack roe and roll in 1/4 sheet of nori. Roll cheese and cucumber in nori for flower center and leaf. Assemble flowers with leaf and roll up.

MAY CARNATION

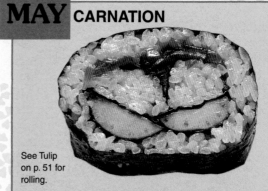

See Tulip on p. 51 for rolling.

Make petals with fukujin-zuke (pickled vegetable slices) and leaves with cucumber. Season rice with curry powder and spread it on nori and roll. You may use takuan and chopped ginger for fukujin-zuke.

MAR JAPANESE QUINCE

See Sasanqua on p. 53 for rolling.

Mix rice with chopped sausage for petals and roll in 1/4 sheet of nori. Make flower center with pokeweed and bud with fukujin-zuke (pickled vegetable slices). Roll in thin omelet seasoned with salt.

JUN THISTLE

See Dandelion on p. 52 for rolling.

Use shibazuke (assorted vegetables hashed and pickled in salt) for bud and chopped shibazuke for flower. Cut cucumber into three lengthwise and use them as leaves. Place fillings on sushi rice and roll in nori.

The climate of Japan is characterized by four distinct seasons, spring, summer, autumn, and winter. People take pleasure in the transition of the seasons. Here are maki-zushi which represent seasonal changes. The changing of the seasons brings us peace of mind in our busy daily lives.

JUL CHERRIES

Roll sausage in 1/3 sheet of nori. Make leaves with cucumber cut into pieces lengthwise. Mix rice with aona-furikake (powder of greens) as desired. Place fillings on rice and roll in nori.

OCT SMALL CHRYSANTHEMUM

See Tulip on p. 51 for rolling

Make petals with thick omelet cut into 3/8" (1 cm) cubes. Cut cucumber into 8 lengthwise and make calyx. Place turnip greens one upon another and make leaves. Place the whole on sushi rice and roll in nori.

AUG SUNFLOWER

See Turban Shell on p. 50 for rolling.

Make petals with thick omelet cut into 3/8" (1 cm) cubes and flower center with cheese rolled in 1/4 sheet of nori. Make bud with cucumber and pokeweed. Place fillings on rice mixed with sesame seeds and roll.

NOV BEAR

See Koala on pp. 62~63 for rolling.

Stir-fry thin meat seasoned as desired. Roll it in 1/3 sheet of nori and make nose. Make eyes with stems of turnip greens and ears with sausages. Mix rice with minced carrot cooked in sugar and roll the whole together in thin omelet.

SEP POPPY

See Sasanqua on p. 53 for rolling.

Mix rice with minced carrot cooked in sugar and roll it in 1/4 sheet of nori, which makes petals. Make flower center with pokeweed and leaf with cucumber. Roll the whole together.

DEC ROSE

See Sasanqua on p. 53 for rolling.

Place ham and sushi rice mixed with cooked egg yolk on 1 sheet of nori and roll in a spiral. Cut cucumber into 8 lengthwise and make leaves. Roll the whole together in nori.

Ingredients

●PINE (for 1 roll)
1 pickled nozawana (turnip greens)
2 wide kanpyo (p. 48)
4 cups sushi rice (p. 48)
1 Tbsp aonori (green seaweed)
1 thin omelet (8 1/4" × 8 1/4" (21 cm × 21 cm))
1 1/2 sheets nori seaweed

●BAMBOO (for 1 roll)
1~2 pickled nozawana (turnip greens)
1~2 pickled pokeweed
4 cups sushi rice (p. 48)
1 Tbsp aonori (green seaweed)
1 thin omelet (8 1/4" × 8 1/4" (21 cm × 21 cm))
1 1/2 sheets nori seaweed

●UME (for 1 roll)
3~4 wide kanpyo (p. 48)
Dash shredded thin omelet
Dash chopped ginger
4 cups sushi rice (p.48)
1 Tbsp sakura-denbu (mashed and seasoned fish)
1 thin omelet (8 1/4" × 8 1/4" (21 cm × 21 cm))
2 sheets nori seaweed

●KARAKUSA (for 1 roll)
1 pickled pokeweed
2 kanpyo (p. 48)
1 1/4 cups sushi rice (p. 48)

●CRANE & TURTLE
2 Eggs

In the central part of Chiba Prefecture, where the author Ms. Mizuno was born, futomaki-zushi (thick rice rolls) was customarily served on ceremonial occasions. For a happy event, rolls of pine, bamboo, and ume was packed in a small wooden box, and rolls of chrysanthemum for a funeral service. It was a part of the essential training for a bride-to-be to learn how to make futomaki. When using nori in place of thin omelet, use 1 1/4 sheets of nori seaweed.

 UME

See Sasanqua on
p. 53 for rolling.

Method: ❶ Combine a small bowl of sushi rice and denbu (mashed and seasoned fish) and mix well. Roll it in 1/5 sheet of nori and make petals. Make the flower center by rolling shredded thin omelet in 1/4 sheet of nori.
❷ Spread the sushi rice on a thin omelet, leaving 1 1/8" (3 cm) open on either ends. Place assembled flowers on it and make a mound on the right and cover with 3/4 sheet of nori. Place minced ginger in the groove and a kanpyo on the right side of the mound. Fold over the nori.
❸ Place the remaining kanpyo on the flowers and cover with the nori folded over. Add the sushi rice and roll.

KARAKUSA, CRANE & TURTLE

Karakusa is an arabesque. Roll the pokeweed at the end of nori. Place the kanpyo beside it. Spread the sushi rice over them, leaving 3/8" (1 cm) open at the end and roll. Make the crane and turtle with boiled eggs. Make patterns with a heated metal skewer. Put red food coloring on the head of the crane.

PINE

Preparation for fillings

Make a thin omelet (8 1/4" x 8 1/4" (21 cm × 21 cm)) with 4 eggs with sugar and salt added as desired. Cut only leaves of nozawana into the same length of omelet (8 1/4" (21 cm)). Cut each leaf into 3 portions. Mix a small bowl of sushi rice with the aonori.

Spread the nozawana in the center of 1/3 sheet of nori and place the rice and aonori mixture on it. Bring both ends of nori together to meet and shape into a triangle. Make three rolls in this way, which represent pine leaves.

Spread the sushi rice thinly on the thin omelet, leaving 1 1/8" (3 cm) open both ends. Place a pine leave in the center with the joint up and make small rice mounds on both sides.

Place the other pine leaves on both rice mounds with the joints directed inwards.

Cover the groove in the center with 3/4" (2 cm)-wide nori and place the kanpyo one upon another. Add the rice on both sides up to the height of pine leaves.

Fold 2 3/4" (7 cm)-wide nori in half and cover the kanpyo. Stick both ends of nori to the rice.

Press lightly from both sides and shape into a round. Holding with one hand, add additional rice.

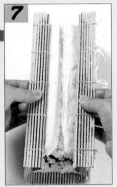

Bring the omelet together and press firmly to form a shape. You may leave the joint of the omelet open.

BAMBOO

Preparation for fillings

Make a thin omelet (8 1/4" × 8 1/4" (21 cm × 21 cm)) with 4 eggs with sugar and salt added as desired. Cut stems and leaves of nozawana into 8 1/4" (21 cm)-lengths. Cut the leaves into 3 portions. Cut thin pokeweeds into 8 1/4" (21 cm)-lengths. Mix a small bowl of sushi rice with the aonori.

Fold 3/8" (1 cm) from the edge of 1/2 sheet of nori. Spread the rice and aonori mixture on the nori, leaving 1/8" (5 mm) open from the fold and 3/8" (1 cm) from the other end. Fold the nozawana leaves in 5/8" (1.5 cm)-widths and place on the left side of the rice.

Place the folded nori on the nozawana and shape into a bamboo leaf as shown. Make three rolls in this way, which represent bamboo leaves.

Spread the sushi rice on a thin omelet, leaving 1 1/8" (3 cm) open at both ends. Assemble the stems of nozawana and pokeweed in the center and place two rolls of leaves on both sides with the joints up.

Holding the bamboo mat with one hand, move the ends of leaves a little inward shapely, and place the other roll on them.

Add the rice between the leaves as shown. Press both sides of the mat and let meet the omelet. Form into a round shape.

ORIGINAL FANCY MAKI-ZUSHI

Children will like the hamburger, the panda and koala rolls.

Hamburger Turtle

Squid Butterfly

Chicken Tulip

HAMBURGER TURTLE

Ingredients (for 1 roll)

Hamburger
- **3 1/2** oz (100 g) beef and pork ground together
- **1/4** onion
- **1/2** egg
- **2** Tbsp bread crumbs
- **1** Tbsp milk
- **2** Tbsp Worcester sauce
- **2** Tbsp tomato ketchup
- **1** cucumber

- **1** lettuce leaf
- **1 1/4** cups sushi rice (p. 48)
- **1** thin omelet (8 1/4" × 7" (21 cm × 18 cm))

Method: ❶ Mince the onion and stir-fry. Combine the bread crumbs and milk. Mix all the ingredients for hamburger together and make a bar a little longer than the length of nori seaweed (8 1/4" (21 cm)). Wrap in oiled alminum foil and cook in the oven. Brown in a frying pan and season with the sauce and ketchup.

❷ Rub the cucumber with salt and cut into 8 lengthwise, of which 5 will be used for the head and legs. Use the lettuce leaf for the tail. (Wrap each in nori to outline.)

❸ Cook a thin omelet with 2 eggs seasoned with salt and pepper.

❹ Spread the sushi rice on the omelet, leaving 1 1/8" (3 cm) open at both ends and roll in the same way as Sasanqua on page 53.

SQUID BUTTERFLY

Ingredients (for 1 roll)

2 squid (bodies)
2~3 pickled pokeweed
1 cucumber
1 1/4 cups sushi rice (p. 48)
1~2 Tbsp yukari (salted and dried shiso leaves, minced)
3 sheets of nori seaweed

1

Place a piece of squid as long as the nori on 2/3 sheet of nori. Dab water at the edge of nori and roll it with the pokeweed in the center. Water helps the nori stick together.

Preparation for fillings

Cut each squid in half, score the surface and broil with salt. Rub the cucumber and cut lengthwise in 1/8" (5 mm) width.

2

Spread the rice mixed with yukari on a sheet of nori, leaving 1 1/8" (3 cm) open at both ends. Add the rice mixture in the center and make a mound 3/8" (1 cm) high.

3

Fold 1/4 sheet of nori in half and cover the mound. Press both ends lightly with a chopstick. This nori makes the antennae of the butterfly.

4

Add the rice mixture gradually on both sides of the mound, so it is a little lower than the mound.

5

On the mound, place two squid rolls (wings) with the cucumber put between. Hold the bamboo mat with both hands and press lightly towards the center. Pass the mat to one hand and add the additional rice with the other hand. Bring the nori to overlap and roll and form into shape.

CHICKEN TULIP

Ingredients (for 1 roll)

1/2 chicken breast
Seasonings
 { 1 Tbsp sugar
 { 1 Tbsp shoyu
 { 1 Tbsp sake
1 cucumber
1 1/4 cups sushi rice (p. 48)
1 thin omelet (8 1/4" × 7" (21 cm × 18 cm))
1 sheet of nori seaweed

Method: ❶ Cut the chicken lengthwise 3/4" (2 cm) square. Heat oil in a frying pan and fry. When the surface has been browned, discard the oil. Add the seasonings and cook to taste salty-sweet. Rub the cucumber with a dash of salt until limp. Cut in half lengthwise.

❷ Cook a thin omelet seasoned with salt and pepper, the same size as a sheet of nori (8 1/4" × 7" (21 cm × 18 cm)).

❸ Place the omelet on a bamboo mat and spread the sushi rice thinly, leaving 3/4" (2 cm) open on both ends. The chicken represents flowers and the cucumber leaves. Roll in the same way as Tulip on page 51. You may leave the joint of the omelet open as shown in the photo.

● PANDA ●

Ingredients (for 1 roll)
10 thin kanpyo (p. 48)
2 1/2 cups sushi rice (p. 48)
3 sheets nori seaweed

Other fillings

In place of kanpyo, you may use any ingredients desired. The photo shows minced conger eel surrounded by rice and parsley mixture. Deep colored fillings may be used without rolling in nori.

Make the Face with Nori and Kanpyo

Ears

Eyes

Nose

Mouth

Prepare one very thin and soft kanpyo and other 9 kanpyo. Twist 2 kanpyo each for ears, and place 2 kanpyo each one upon another and cut into 3/8" (1 cm) widths for eyes. Use the very thin kanpyo for the nose. Cut one kanpyo into 3/8" (1 cm) widths for the mouth.

First make the face. Spread the sushi rice thinly in the center about 1 1/8" (3 cm) wide on a 4" (10 cm)-wide nori. Place the mouth with the kanpyo down.

Add the rice thinly over the mouth. This rice makes a space between the mouth and nose.

Place the thin nose in the center with the jo down.

Spread the sushi rice thinly on a sheet of nori, leaving 1 1/8" (3 cm) open at both ends. Make two grooves in the center at intervals of 1 1/2" (4 cm) with moistened chopsticks.

Double the nori of the ear and place between the grooves and open right and left.

To make a groove for the kanpyo, push the no down with chopsticks in the groove made ⑦.

Cut the nori into 3 1/2" (9 cm) width.
Roll together with the kanpyo.
Cut all the nori beforehand into the
widths designated.

Sandwich the kanpyo with the nori
1 3/8" (3.5 cm) wide.

Roll a very thin and soft kanpyo in
the nori 1 1/8" (3 cm) wide.

Place the kanpyo 3/8" (1 cm) wide
on the nori 3/8" (1 cm) wide.

5

6

...d the rice on both sides of the nose little by
...le in a triangle shape. Stick the eyes a little
...low the top of the triangles.

Spread the rice thinly over the eyes and cover
them, taking care not to break down the triangles.

Holding both sides of the bamboo mat, press
lightly toward the center to form a shape like a
full-cheeked face. Leave the edges of the nori
open as shown in the photo.

11

12

...vist two kanpyo into one and place each in
...e grooves to make ears.

Place the face upside down between the ears.
Holding the bamboo mat on both sides, press
lightly toward the center to form a round shape.

Holding the mat with the left hand, add additional rice with the right hand over the under
part of the face to cover the nori. Join the nori
together and form into desired shape.

● KOALA ●

Ingredients (for 1 roll)
1 3/4 oz (50 g) roast pork
1~2 cheese kamaboko
(steamed fish & cheese paste cake)
1 1/4 cups sushi rice (p. 48)
1 1/4 cups fried rice
1 thin omelet (8 1/4" × 7"
(21 cm × 18 cm))
2 sheets nori seaweed

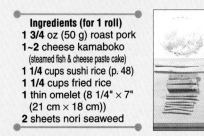

Preparation of fillings

Cut the roast pork into sticks, 3/8" (1 cm) square to make the nose, and 1/8" (5 mm) square to make the eyes. They are lined up the full length of the nori (8 1/4" (21 cm)). Cut the cheese kamaboko into half lengthwise to make the ears, 8 1/4" (21 cm) long. Stir-fry the rice seasoned as desired. Cook a thin omelet with two eggs seasoned with salt and pepper in the size directed.

Place the roast pork sticks cut into 1/8" (5 mm) square on 1/6 sheet nori, joining as long as the nori and roll with the bamboo mat. Make two of them for the eyes. Roll the roast sticks cut into 3/8" (1 cm) square in the same way for the nose.

1

Head of the koala. Spread the sushi rice thinly in 1 1/8" (3 cm) wide in the center of 2/3 sheet of nori. Add the rice and make a mound in the center as if the grains are aligned. This mound separates the eyes. Place the eyes on both sides of the mound.

2

Add the rice a bit at a time over the eye high as the center mound. This rice fills space between the eyes and nose.

5

Spread the fried rice on a sheet of the thin omelet, leaving 1 1/8" (3 cm) open on both ends.

6

Make two grooves with moistened chopsticks in the rice, leaving 1 1/2" (4 cm) space in the center between them. Ears are placed in these grooves.

7

To make distinct outlines of the ears, pre two sheets of 1/4 nori. Place each nori on grooves and lightly push in.

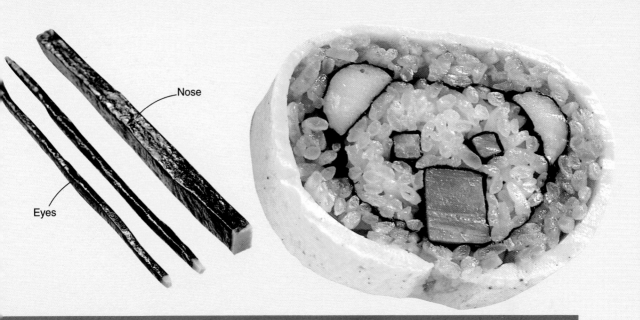

Nose

Eyes

Place the bar of the nose with the joint up in the center. Add the rice a bit at a time on both sides of the nose as high as the nose. Take care not to place the rice on the nose, as shown in the photo.

4

Hold both sides of the bamboo mat with hands and roll toward the center. Join the edges of the nori on the nose and form into a round shape.

Place the cheese kamaboko on each groove, with the cut side slanted inward, to make nicely shaped ears.

9

Place the face made in ④ upside down between the ears. Holding the bamboo mat with both hands, press lightly toward the center and roll to form a cylinder.

10

Hold the mat with the left hand, and add additional fried rice and roll. Adjust the shape with the joint down.

MAKI-ZUSHI
(Rolled Sushi)

Fillings
A colorful assortment of ingredients such as kanpyo, omelet, sakura-denbu (mashed and seasoned fish), mitsuba (honewort), pickled greens, and shiitake mushrooms.

Method: ❶ Place a sheet of nori seaweed on a bamboo mat horizontally. Spread the sushi rice, leaving a margin of 3/8" (1 cm) at the end nearest you and 3/4" (2 cm) at the farther end.
❷ With color in mind, place the fillings in the center of the rice one upon another.
❸ Starting at the edge closer to you, bring the nori over the fillings toward the opposite end. Take care so that the fillings do not fall apart.
❹ Join the front rice with the rice on the opposite side and press lightly from above.
❺ Turning the mat back toward you (photo 3), roll up. Place the roll with the seam down and shape it.

HOSOMAKI-ZUSHI
(Thin Rolled Sushi)

Fillings
Kanpyo (Teppo-maki), tuna (Tekka-maki), and cucumber (Kappa-maki) are popular. Pickled ume, aojiso (green shiso leaves), salmon roe, mitsuba (honewort), and natto (fermented soybeans) are also used.

Methods: Spread the sushi rice on the nori cut in half horizontally. Place the fillings as desired and roll up.
Cutting:
The rules for cutting hosomaki-zushi are to cut a roll of teppo-maki into four portions and the tekka- and kappa-maki into six.